IT'S a MUSICaL!

400 Questions to Ponder, Discuss, and Fight About

by Scott Miller
musical theatre composer,
lyricist, bookwriter, historian,
consultant, fanboy, and
artistic director of New Line Theatre

© 2016

Books by Scott Miller
From Assassins to West Side Story
Deconstructing Harold Hill
Rebels with Applause
Let the Sun Shine In: The Genius of HAIR
Strike Up the Band: A New History of Musical Theatre
Sex, Drugs, Rock & Roll, and Musicals
In the Blood, a novel

Musicals by Scott Miller
Adam's Apple
Musical
Topsiders
The Line
Astro Turf
Attempting the Absurd
Breaking Out in Harmony
In the Blood
Johnny Appleweed
The Zombies of Penzance

Plays by Scott Miller
Head Games
A Hot Cup of Murder

What's the Use of Wonderin'?

This book is filled with 400 questions designed to make the serious musical theatre fanboy and fangirl think about musicals, how they operate, how they interact with each other and with the Real World, how they are related, how they have and haven't changed over the years, what they have been and what they are becoming in this new Golden Age of the American Musical Theatre.

You can flip through this book, land on any page, read a question, and test yourself on your knowledge, insights, and opinions about musicals. Or you can make it a game (see below) with your similarly obsessed friends. Or you can use it to humiliate posers who only pretend to know our art form. Your choice. *But wield your power carefully.*

The primary purpose here is just for serious, hardcore, musical theatre fans to have lots of musical theatre fun with other serious, hardcore, musical theatre fans. Or with themselves. *But remember – alone is alone, not alive.*

The Time-Honored Way the Game Is Played

These questions appear in random order. Each player takes a question, and if they can't answer it to the group's satisfaction, that player is out. If they answer it successfully, the next question goes to the next player. Play until one player remains.

OR… one player asks the other player(s) questions continuously until the other(s) can't answer one and loses. Then they swap roles. The goal is to get the longest uninterrupted string of legit answers. If there are disputes, the mob rules.

OR… just answer the questions yourself, because you're just that knowledgeable, and enjoy thinking about this amazing time in this new Golden Age of the American musical theatre.

Name a theatre song that always puts you in a good mood.

Name a strong black leading character in a musical.

Quote one dialogue line from a musical that totally encapsulates that show.

Name your favorite Act II opener.

Name a theatre song in which the singer is lying.

Take the title of a famous musical and invent a completely different plot synopsis for it.

Name a mixed drink mentioned in a musical.

What musical would be hardest to explain to someone who knew nothing about it?

Name your favorite Kander & Ebb vamp.

Name a theatre song that mentions June.

Invent one of the Ten Commandments of Musical Theatre.

Name the sexiest character (not the actor) in a musical.

Name a theatre song that mentions food in the title.

Name a musical that features non-human characters.

Name a musical set in New Jersey.

Name a theatre song with the word "home" in the title.

Name a musical in which one or more of the main characters is dead by the end of the show.

Name a musical that deals directly with the issue of race.

Name a show that references Shakespeare in one way or another.

Name someone really talented in your own community, along with the perfect musical theatre role for them.

Name a theatre song with the word "may" in the title.

Name a theatre song that would be terrible for a wedding ceremony.

Re-title a famous musical as if it were about stoners.

Name a musical for every letter of your full name.

Give us a bold, new concept for an existing musical. Wrong answers only.

What's the worst musical you ever saw on or off Broadway?

If you could have a musical theatre related super power, what would it be?

Name the most emotional moment you've ever experienced in a musical.

What musical would make a great themed restaurant?

Name a musical that has a party scene.

Name a theatre song title that might sound obscene out of context.

Name a musical theatre character who is cruel.

Name your Top Five theatre songs from the 1990s.

Name an artist of color who's your musical theatre hero.

Re-title a theatre song as if the character singing it is a cat.

What's the best love song ever written for a musical?

Name a musical that would make a great Twilight Zone episode.

You're trapped in an elevator with two musical theatre characters. Who would you prefer?

Name a musical you'd like to slap a moratorium on, so it would not be produced anymore.

If you were a show tune, which one would you be?

Come up with the title of a musical theatre prequel you'd like to see.

Name a novel you've read that is the source material for a stage musical.

Name your favorite musical about African American life.

Name the single most amazing year in the history of musical theatre.

Name two characters from different musicals who would hate each other.

Pick a musical theatre character and assign them a New Year's resolution.

What would be a great musical theatre role for Homer Simpson?

Name a stage musical that would be really great as a big budget movie.

Name a theatre song with the word "new" in it.

Pick a musical theater character – what would be the perfect Christmas present for them?

What's the first musical you saw on Broadway?

Name a theatre song that mentions hot weather.

Name a great musical you saw for the first time this year.

You're going into Witness Relocation and you can only take 3 cast albums: a Sondheim show, a pre-'65 show, and a post-2000 show. Which shows do you take?

What cast album do you listen to when you want to cheer up?

Name a theatre song that became a commercial jingle.

What theatre song can bring you to tears?

Name a theatre song that mentions an animal's name?

Name a legendary flop musical that you would love to see produced now.

What's the oddest musical you've ever seen?

Cast a famous Shakespeare role or roles with musical theatre characters.

Name two characters from different musicals who should really be a couple.

Name a musical theatre character who has served in the armed forces.

Name a musical theater character who is a scientist.

What's the most conventional musical you've ever seen?

Name a theatre song about growing up.

They've written a musical about your life. What's your first "I Want" song called?

Name the three musicals that would tell us everything we need to know about you.

Offer your best advice to someone just starting out in the musical theatre.

Replace one word in the title of a musical with food.

Who is the hardest-rocking character in a musical?

Name your favorite Jewish character in a musical.

Give an example of a deus ex machina in a musical.

Name a theatre lyric that mentions a car brand.

Ruin a musical title with one letter. (Ex. Sunday in the Dark with George, Nair)

Name a cool older musical that more young people should get to know.

Name a musical theatre character who'd be your sworn enemy.

Summarize the plot to a famous musical in three words.

What's the best theatre song to listen to when you're sad?

Name a theatre lyric that mentions the word "summer."

You just inherited a huge amount of money – what show will you produce (or revive) on Broadway?

What musical would be awesome "On Ice"?

Name a musical that's a guilty pleasure.

Name the most interesting father character in a musical.

Name a musical about a (real or fictional) musical.

Name your favorite theatre song with a one-word title.

Name a musical that captures something fundamental about America in the 20th century.

Name the worst mother in a musical.

What musical theatre artist, living or dead, who's not a performer, would you like to have dinner with? And you can't pick Sondheim.

Name a theatre song with the word "new" in it.

If you could pick anyone in the world to sing you a theatre song, who would it be?

If you could force the President to watch one musical, what would it be?

Name a musical in which marijuana is used or mentioned.

Write a Buzzfeed type "click-bait" headline to get people to explore a particular musical.

Name an Irish character in a musical.

Name a musical theatre character who could legit be called a philosopher.

What is your earliest memory related to musical theatre?

What's the saddest love song from a musical that you've ever heard?

Name a theatre lyric that you initially misheard. How long did you sing it the wrong way?

Tell us something about yourself that makes you a musical theatre superfan.

Name a musical you LOVE that you had never heard of one year ago.

Name your favorite African American character in a musical.

Name three characters from three different musicals that you'd like to have Thanksgiving dinner with.

Name a musical with a one-word title.

Name your favorite gay character in a musical.

What is the first cast album you bought for yourself? (No soundtracks!)

If you had to pick one Anything Goes – 1934, 1962, 1987, or 2011?

Name a musical with "no" or "not" in the title.

What do you think is the most famous theatre song among non-theatre people?

Name a musical you discovered and fell in love with during the past year.

Name a musical that contains a celebration.

Name a musical that opened on Broadway the year you were born.

Who should write the book, music, and lyrics of your bio-musical?

What's the funniest theatre song about love?

Name a musical theatre character who would probably vote Republican.

Write a haiku giving the plot synopsis of a musical:
(5 syllables,
7 syllables,
5 syllables).

Name a musical whose title starts with "The."

If you had a six-hour drive ahead of you, what cast albums would you bring along?

Name a musical that you've just recently discovered (old or new) that is really wonderful.

Name a musical theatre character who's a prostitute.

Name a musical based on the Faust legend.

Remove one letter from the title of a musical, to make a new title.

Name a theatre song about marriage.

Name a musical set in the future.

How many titles of musicals can you get into a single sentence?

Name a theatre song that inspires you.

Write a limerick about a famous musical.

Name a musical that has at least one scene set on July 4.

What's on your list of the Great American Musicals (no more than ten)?

Name a musical in which hairstyle is an important plot element.

Name a theatre song about starting something.

Invent a weird, random fact about a famous musical theatre character.

Name a musical theatre character who works in law enforcement.

Name a musical theatre character who is exactly like one of your best friends (and name the friend).

Name a rock musical set in a period before rock and roll.

Name a musical in which there is an explosion.

Fill in the blank: "My personal hell would be performing in [name a musical] for a year."

Come up with a definition of the new verb, "to musical," and use it in a sentence.

Name an amazing musical that virtually nobody knows about.

Change the title of a famous musical so that it reflects an all-gay cast.

Name a really famous or popular musical that you've never seen.

Name a theatre song about dealing with death.

Confess to a musical theatre heresy you've committed.

What's the oldest musical you've ever seen?

Name a theatre song with the word "You" in it.

If you could only perform in one musical, the same musical, for the rest of your life, what would it be?

Name a musical you consider a masterpiece.

Name a musical theatre character who's in college.

Name a musical in which someone gets stabbed.

What's your favorite theatre lyric with the word "fuck" in it?

Name your favorite opening words or lines in a musical.

Quote a line of spoken dialogue that can be heard on a cast album.

Name a musical theatre character who's clergy.

Name the one song that best exemplifies Stephen Sondheim.

Name a theatre song about ending or the end of something.

In the spirit of Festivus, what's your musical theatre grievance?

Name a rock album that should be a stage musical.

Name a musical set in Africa.

Name a non-"family" musical from which Disney would make a great film adaptation.

Name an act of generosity in a musical.

Pick a musical theatre character and invent a dark secret they're hiding.

Name a family in a musical that you would like to have Thanksgiving dinner with.

Name a theatre lyric with the phrase "thank you" in it.

Name a musical theatre love triangle. Real or fictional.

Name a person who wrote the book, music, and lyrics for a musical.

If you could travel back in time to watch the rehearsal process for one famous musical, which would it be?

Name a manic theatre song.

What's your favorite alliteration in a musical theatre lyric?

Name a musical thriller.

If you had to live inside a musical for the rest of your life, which musical would you pick?

Come up with a title for a new musical about the Tony Awards.

Name three musical theatre characters you'd: 1. hang out with, 2. have sex with, and 3. marry.

Name a really huge musical theatre Fail.

Name a theatre song about a particular job, and songs from Working don't count.

Pair up a recent US Presidential candidate with the musical theatre character most like them.

Which musical gives us the most valuable life lesson(s)?

Take the title of a theatre song and replace one word in it with "bacon."

What musical title has a woman's name in it?

Name a musical theatre character who would make a great Bond villain.

What musical theatre character should be an action figure?

Name your favorite plot twist in a musical.

Name your favorite underdog in a musical.

Is there a musical you really liked the first time you saw or heard it, but that you've grown to dislike over time?

Name a musical thriller.

What musical theatre character's name would make a great pet name?

Cast your favorite cartoon character in the lead in a musical.

Name your favorite movie musical that has never been a stage musical.

Name an all-male group number in a musical (all-male musicals don't count).

What's your favorite sexual innuendo in a theatre lyric?

Name a theatre song about the weekend.

Quote a theatre lyric about America.

Name a theatre song about something surprising happening.

Name a theatre song about being independent, out on your own, free of others' rules or opinions.

Name the funniest musical you've ever seen.

Name the wildest character in musical theatre.

Name two musical theatre characters of the same gender who should definitely get married.

Pick a decade, then name the one musical that exemplifies that decade.

Name a theatre song about being a father.

Name 7 musical theatre characters who illustrate the Seven Deadly Sins: wrath, greed, sloth, pride, lust, envy, gluttony.

If you had a time machine, which musical theatre opening night would you attend?

Name a musical that uses a bed onstage.

Name a musical theatre "earworm," a melody you just can't get out of your head.

Name a theatre song in which exactly three characters are singing.

Name a theatre song about cold.

Name a theatre song title that aptly describes auditioning for a show.

Name the theatre song that most quickly puts you in a good mood.

Name a greatly under-appreciated theatre song.

Name a stage musical Tim Burton should film in stop-motion.

Pick an iconic theatre song and re-assign it to another musical theatre character in a different musical.

Name your favorite musical that debuted before you were born.

You have to cast Donald Trump as a lead in a musical – what role?

Which mother in a musical is most like your mother?

Name a musical theatre character who'd be better off if they'd just smoke a joint and relax.

What's the biggest shock you've ever had, seeing a musical?

Name a theatre song with a color in the title.

Name a theatre song with a number in the title.

Name a musical you saw that was totally different from what you expected.

Name a title character in a musical.

Name a musical theatre role Barbra Streisand would be great for, right now, at this age.

Name a musical based on the Bible.

Pick a musical theatre character and give them a specific superpower that fits them.

Name a theatre song that mentions a US President by name... that isn't from Assassins.

Name a powerful woman character in a musical.

Name a theatre song title that contains at least one word in Latin.

Name a theatre song that has an obscenity in the title.

If aliens visited you, what musical would you take them to, to best explain our culture to them?

Name an animal (real or fake) that appears in a musical.

If The Daily Show were a musical (and really, it should be), who would be the best choice for host?

Rewrite the ending of a famous musical, so the antagonist wins.

Name the most under-appreciated musical.

If the world was about to end, but you had just enough time to listen to one cast album, which one would it be?

Name a musical theatre character that you really hate.

Name a musical theatre character who inspires you.

What's your favorite surprising or "trick" rhyme in a musical?

What musical has had the most profound effect on you?

Name the best song Stephen Schwartz ever wrote.

What was your greatest musical theatre experience of the past year?

What's the most emotional musical you've ever seen?

Name a musical theatre role that Jesus would be right for.

Name a theatre song with a question mark in the title.

What's the most intense musical you've ever seen?

Name a musical theatre character of a different race from you, that you would love to play.

Name a musical theatre character you'd love to go on a date with.

Name a theatre song with a man's name in the title.

What would be the title of a musical about your best friend's life, and who should write it?

Who is someone working in the musical theatre, still living, that you think of as a role model, personally and/or professionally?

Name a musical that you think is partly or entirely autobiographical.

Are we living in a new Golden Age of American musical theatre? What's the evidence?

Match a musical theatre actor of color and a perfect, usually "white" role for them.

Name your favorite theatre song that introduces a character.

Name a theatre song that has the word "I" in it.

Give a musical theatre character a new job.

Name the strongest female character in a musical.

Name a musical theatre character who never appears onstage.

Name a line or phrase from Shakespeare that's in a musical.

Name the best song Kander & Ebb ever wrote.

Name a great song cut from a musical.

Take the title of a theatre song and replace one word in it with a fruit or vegetable.

What news event of the past year would make a great musical? Assign a writing team and/or director.

Name a musical with gun(s) in it.

Take two titles of musicals that a share a common word or phrase and mash them up to make a new title. (Examples: The Sound of Music Man, The Lion King and I...)

Name a musical set in the 1930s.

Name a theatre song about time.

Name a musical about a predator.

Name four characters from four different musicals who would make an awesome dinner party.

Name a theatre song that would take on an interesting new meaning if it were put in Rent.

Name a theatre song about being thankful or grateful.

Name a theatre song with the word "December" in it.

Name your favorite sidekick in a musical.

Name a character or a couple from a musical that belong on The Jerry Springer Show.

Name a character in a musical who works in law enforcement.

Name a theatre song about light.

Quote a phrase or sentence from a musical theatre lyric that makes a great Wise Saying. (Anything from Into the Woods doesn't count.)

Name a musical that most people hate but that you love.

Name a musical that most people love but that you hate.

Name a theatre lyric with the word "want" (or wants, wanting, wanted, etc.) in it.

Name the best song Sondheim ever wrote.

Pick a title of an existing musical that would also make a great title for a musical about your life.

Name a musical in which the time and/or place is pretty much a central character itself.

Name your favorite theatre composer-lyricist team, past or present.

Name a strong Asian character in a musical.

Name the Tony Award winning Best Musical of 2024.

Name a musical theatre term or concept that non-musical-theatre folks probably don't know or understand.

Name a theatre song whose title aptly describes American politics right now.

Name a musical with punctuation in its title.

Name a musical with an anti-hero for a protagonist.

Name any musical and one sentence that describes the central point –not the plot – of the show.

Name a musical with a person's name in the title.

What's your favorite theatre song to sing?

What's the most interesting character name in any musical?

Name your one –only one – all-time favorite musical theatre artist (actor, writer, composer, director, choreographer, whatever) still alive today.

Name a musical theatre character who would make the worst advice columnist ever.

Name a pair of "opposites" in a musical (i.e., Javert and Valjean, Laurey and Ado Annie).

Name your Top Five Desert Island Musicals.

Name a musical that starts and ends with the same song (even if it's different lyrics).

Name a truly great opening number in a musical.

Cast the leading roles if Star Trek were to become a stage musical.

Pick an existing musical and assign a different writer or writing team to it (i.e., West Side Story, Lin-Manuel Miranda; or The Wild Party, Bill Finn).

Name a theatre song that describes your day today.

Finish this sentence: "Dear American Musical Theatre, I wish..."

Cast your favorite musical theatre actor (in New York or elsewhere) in a role they haven't played yet.

Name a musical that takes place (at least partly) on the night before a holiday.

Invent a new musical theatre term and give us a definition.

Name a theatre song that prominently involves numbers (i.e., "Tea for Two" or "Seasons of Love").

Name a dance introduced in a musical (i.e., "The Time Warp").

Name a troubled father character in a musical.

Name a musical with a character named Ben or Benny.

Name a musical set entirely
or partly in Texas.

Name an a cappella number
in a musical.

Is your favorite musical
today the same as your
favorite musical five years
ago? Ten years ago? What
are/were they?

What's your favorite one or
two lines from a musical
theatre lyric?

Name a mother character from a musical that you would love to have as your own mother.

Name a musical theatre reference to baseball.

Name a character in a musical who never appears onstage.

Name a title of a musical that doesn't really tell you much at all about the story or premise.

Come up with an alternate title for Rent.

Name a musical theatre role that was originally cast with one actor, but then recast before opening on or off Broadway.

Name a theatre song about Spring.

What's your favorite musical that debuted in the 1990s?

Name a musical in which a major character is sick and/or dying.

What is the most important aspect of a successful musical?

Name a musical theatre actor you've seen on any of the Law & Order series.

What's the coolest piece of musical theatre you saw live in the past five years?

What stage musical has the best title?

Fill in the blank –"The state of the American musical theatre is
_____."

How old were you when you saw our first musical, and what show was it?

What's the last theatre song that was in your head?

Pick one line of lyric from a theatre song that would make a great epitaph for you.

Name your favorite Jewish character in a musical.

Take two or more titles of musicals that can be combined to form a complete sentence.

Name a musical theatre character who's in the military.

Choose a phrase from a musical theatre lyric that would make a great catch-phrase for a commercial product.

Name a musical you think just didn't work, and assign a different writer or team to it.

Name a horror movie you'd love to see onstage as a musical.

Come up with a new title for an existing musical.

Quote a theatre lyric from before 1960 that you think is particularly truthful.

Name the most brilliant rhyme you've ever heard in a musical.

Name your favorite musical that's never played Broadway.

What musical theatre character would make a great Batman?

Cast Rent using only the Muppets.

Name your favorite grandparent in a musical.

Name a specific date mentioned in a musical, i.e. (May 20 is Eliza Doolittle Day, according to "Just You Wait").

Cast The Music Man using only superheroes.

What musical would be cooler if one of its characters were a zombie? And which character...?

Take a character from a musical and cast him/her in a role in Into the Woods.

Come up with the title and a one-sentence plot synopsis for a new sequel to a famous musical.

Name a theatre song whose title does not contain an A or an E.

Name a black musical you haven't seen but would love to.

Name a theatre song that references July 4th.

Name your favorite theatre song that tells a self-contained story.

Name your favorite musical theatre list song.

Who's your favorite Rocky Horror character and why?

If the President had to give his State of the Union address in the form of a theatre song (and how awesome would that be!), what song would it be...?

Name a theatre song about politics.

Name your favorite musical that you consider "adult."

What's the first musical you were ever in, where, and when?

Name the funniest song you've ever heard in a musical.

Name a real person who's also a character in a musical.

The Book of Mormon ads include a press quote saying it's the best musical in the last 25 years. Can you think of a better musical in the last 25 years?

Name a theatre song that mentions a bodily fluid.

Name a musical in which Jesus is a character.

Name a famous person whose life would make a terrible musical comedy.

What's the most R-rated stage musical you've ever seen?

Name a character from a musical you'd like to have in Congress right now.

Name a character in a musical, besides Diana Goodman, who's probably bipolar.

What's the strangest love song you can think of from a musical?

Name a theatre song that mentions snow.

Name a musical that represents your life today.

In many musicals, the hero has to either assimilate into the community or be removed from it by the end. Name a musical in which the hero assimilates.

Name a theatre song about heat.

Name a musical that celebrates racial and/or sexual diversity.

What's the coolest musical you saw in the last year?

Name a musical that a young director could learn a lot from directing – and why.

Name a theatre song that contains the word, "Halloween."

Name one musical – only one – that you are genuinely grateful for.

Name the Top Five Movies That Should Be Musicals.

Who would be the best writer or team to write Dexter: The Musical?

Name the one musical you've never seen that you would most like to see.

Name an old movie that should be a stage musical.

Name a musical in which a real American President is a character.

If you have a pet, what (human) musical theatre role would they be perfect in?

Come up with a title for a new rock musical based on a current/recent political figure.

Name a character in a musical who you'd love to discuss theatre with.

What's the coolest part you've ever played in a musical?

Name a musical that involves a political campaign.

Pick two characters from musicals who would be an awesome Presidential/Vice Presidential ticket.

Name your favorite musical about a real person or people.

Think of a famous person and a musical that would teach him/her something they need to learn.

Name your Top Five Favorite Musical Comedies.

Name a musical and a famous person who should never star in it.

Name a musical that is just too "politically incorrect" to be produced anymore.

Name a musical in which football figures in the plot.

Name a musical that's essentially a Romeo & Juliet star-crossed lovers story... other than West Side Story...

Name a TV sitcom that would make a great musical.

Name a musical based on a foreign film.

Name a musical based on a Shakespeare play.

Name a musical that fills you with joy.

It is 1,000 years in the future and one American musical from this era has somehow become the basis for a new worldwide religion. Which show should it be...?

Made in the USA
Middletown, DE
09 December 2019